Keys to Stylistic Mastery

28 Late Elementary to Early Intermediate Pieces from Five Style Periods

Ingrid Jacobson Clarfield
Dennis Alexander

- Melody
- Technique
- Rhythm
- Dynamics
- Harmony
- Expression
- Tempo
- Ornamentation
- Texture
- Pedal

*This book is dedicated to Dr. Gary L. Ingle, whose friendship
and professional support we both value.*

*We extend our heartfelt appreciation to Kelly Setler Scheer
for her creativity and incredible amount of work on this project.*

*We would like to express gratitude to the others who provided assistance
during various phases of preparing this book:
Dean Elder, Tom Gerou, E. L. Lancaster, Amanda Clarfield Newell,
Kim Newman, Chisato Oey and Stephen Sharp.*

Alfred Music Publishing Co., Inc.
P.O. Box 10003
Van Nuys, CA 91410-0003
alfred.com

ISBN-10: 0-7390-3027-2
ISBN-13: 978-0-7390-3027-1

TABLE OF CONTENTS

For the Teacher 3

For the Student 3

THE BAROQUE PERIOD 4

Alexander, Dennis . . . . *March in G Major* 6

Lully, Jean-Baptiste . . . . *Menuet in D Minor* 7

Krieger, Johann . . . . *Menuett in A Minor* 8

Telemann, Georg Philipp . . . . *Gigue* 10

Bach, Johann Sebastian . . . . *Chorale* 11

Handel, George Frideric . . . . *Aylesford Piece* 12

THE CLASSICAL PERIOD 14

Diabelli, Anton . . . . *Bagatelle* 16

Neefe, Christian Gottlob . . . . *Kanzonette in C Major* 17

Czerny, Carl . . . . *Melody in G Major* 18

Sonata-Allegro Form 19

Alexander, Dennis . . . . *Miniature Sonatina* 20

Steibelt, Daniel . . . . *Adagio* 22

Haydn, Franz Joseph . . . . *German Dance in G Major* 24

THE ROMANTIC PERIOD 26

Breslaur, Emil . . . . *Waltz* 28

Alexander, Dennis . . . . *Tender Thoughts* 29

Schumann, Robert . . . . *Little Piece* 30

Reinecke, Carl . . . . *Elegy* 31

Gurlitt, Cornelius . . . . *March* 32

Thomé, François . . . . *Melody* 34

THE IMPRESSIONIST PERIOD 36

Alexander, Dennis . . . . *Glistening Willows* 38

Alexander, Dennis . . . . *Osaka Castle Gardens* 39

Alexander, Dennis . . . . *Temple Bells* 40

Alexander, Dennis . . . . *The Lonely Sparrow* 41

THE CONTEMPORARY PERIOD 42

Stravinsky, Igor . . . . *Andantino* 44

Bartók, Béla . . . . *Hungarian Folk Dance* 45

Maykapar, Samuel . . . . *The Shepherd's Flute* 46

Rebikov, Vladimir . . . . *The Chinese Doll* 47

Bartók, Béla . . . . *Slovak Peasant's Dance* 48

Alexander, Dennis . . . . *Zany Zebras* 50

About the Composers 52

Glossary 54

About the Authors 56

FOR THE TEACHER

The Purpose of This Book

This book is designed to teach the basic principles of the five stylistic periods (Baroque, Classical, Romantic, Impressionist, and Contemporary) to piano students. The pieces were chosen to provide a helpful transition from method books to the classics. Students will learn to apply stylistic principles directly to these pieces and can then apply them to other music.

Choice of Music and Sequencing

This book includes music from the five stylistic periods—some by famous composers, others by less familiar composers. Repertoire was selected for its musical appeal and effectiveness in conveying the stylistic traits of the period.

Composer Dennis Alexander has written at least one piece in the style of each period. All pieces representing the Impressionist period were written by Mr. Alexander, since Impressionist composers did not write pieces at this level.

The pieces are arranged in approximate order of difficulty within each period. Students should work on pieces from the different style periods simultaneously, comparing similarities and differences.

Editorial Suggestions

Each piece appears in its original form with editorial suggestions. Since Baroque and Classical composers provided few fingerings, dynamics, articulations, or tempo indications, most of the suggestions for these periods are editorial. Composers from the Romantic and Contemporary periods were more specific, but some editorial suggestions are also included for these pieces. Indications such as *f*-*p* mean that the section is to be played *f* the first time and *p* on the repeat.

Metronome markings are suggested in a wide range to allow students to find a tempo at which they can comfortably perform the music artistically.

 # FOR THE STUDENT

What Is Style?

In music, art, or literature, style is usually divided into five periods: Baroque, Classical, Romantic, Impressionist and Contemporary. Each period has its own specific characteristics. Knowledge of these traits will help you learn and perform the music. It is also helpful to learn about composers and the periods and countries in which they lived. Combine this with information about other arts, and you will possess the "Keys to Stylistic Mastery."

How to Use This Book

Information about each style period precedes the music from that period. This section lists selected composers, keyboard instruments and typical forms from the period. It also contains a section called *Keys to Stylistic Mastery* that will aid you in learning and performing in a stylistic manner.

The *Keys to Stylistic Mastery* section is divided into general categories such as melody, rhythm, harmony, tempo, texture, technique, dynamics, expression, ornamentation and pedal. Basic stylistic characteristics are listed in bold under each general category. Many of these characteristics will be found in the music you are studying, but all traits may not be present in every piece. The "keys" listed below each basic stylistic characteristic suggest specific ways to apply this information to the music.

Read these pages about the style period before you begin a new piece and apply this information to the piece that you are studying. In addition, at the top of each page of music there is a section called "Keys to This Piece" found in a shaded box. These "Keys" apply specifically to the piece that follows and reinforce information found in the more general *Keys to Stylistic Mastery* section.

Selected words that might require further explanation are written in ***bold italics*** in the text. These words are defined in the Glossary on pages 54 and 55.

Enjoy studying and playing pieces from all five style periods using these "keys" that lead to stylistic mastery.

THE BAROQUE PERIOD

(1600–1750)

Composers

Johann Sebastian Bach (1685–1750)

François Couperin (1668–1733)

George Frideric Handel (1685–1759)

Jean-Baptiste Lully (1632–1687)

Jean-Philippe Rameau (1683–1764)

Domenico Scarlatti (1685–1757)

Georg Philipp Telemann (1681–1767)

Keyboard Instruments

Clavichord

Harpsichord

Organ

Typical Forms

Invention

Fugue

Toccata

Prelude

March

Dance

KEYS TO STYLISTIC MASTERY

Melody

Includes short *motives,* often repeated starting on another pitch.

🔑 Vary dynamics when *motive* repeats.

Choice of *articulation* affects the *character.*

🔑 In general, play stepwise motion *legato* and play skips and upbeats detached.

Rhythm

Often based on popular dance steps.

🔑 Learn about the dance so you can understand how the steps affect the rhythm.

Harmony

Written in major or minor keys with shifts to *closely related keys.*

🔑 Identify the key of each section to help you learn and memorize the piece.

🔑 Warm up with a scale in the key of the piece. This will help you remember sharps or flats in the key and to hear the *tonality.*

Tempo

Must be steady, often with a slight *ritardando* at the final cadence.

🔑 Learn the music using a metronome.

🗝 Texture

Usually *linear,* with both hands being equally important.

🗝 Learn the music hands separately (HS) to hear each voice independently.

Counterpoint is frequently used.

🗝 Practice each melody separately; keep the *articulation* the same each time it appears.

🗝 Technique

Often requires different touches in each hand.

🗝 Listen for the different touches when one hand is *legato* and the other is detached.

Sound should be clear and precise.

🗝 Keep fingertips firm for a clear sound.

🗝 Dynamics

Usually not provided by the composer, but should be added. *Terraced dynamics* are effective when patterns repeat.

🗝 Look for patterns in the music and add your own dynamics to create echo effects or *terraced dynamics* when the patterns repeat.

Range should be between *p* and *f* to reflect the sounds of Baroque keyboards.

🗝 *Piano* must be delicate, but not thin; *forte* should be bright, but not harsh.

🗝 Expression

Contains one specific feeling or mood. Often reflects the *character* of a dance.

🗝 Learn the meaning of the title to help determine the mood. Expression must be subtle.

🗝 Ornamentation

Makes melodies more expressive, sustains the sound, and provides variety on repeats.

🗝 First learn the piece without the *ornaments.* Practice *ornaments* separately and add them to the music when you feel secure.

🗝 Start all *ornaments* on the beat.

🗝 Pedal

Generally not used, but *damper pedal* can be added for a gentle emphasis on long notes. The *una corda (u.c.)* pedal may be used for an echo effect.

🗝 First learn without pedal, and listen where light pedal might be effective on a long note or where *una corda* might be used for an echo.

March in G Major

Dennis Alexander (b. 1947)

Allegro robusto (♩ = 120–144)
(Quickly, with a bold character)

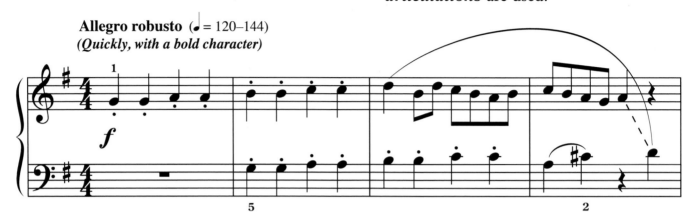

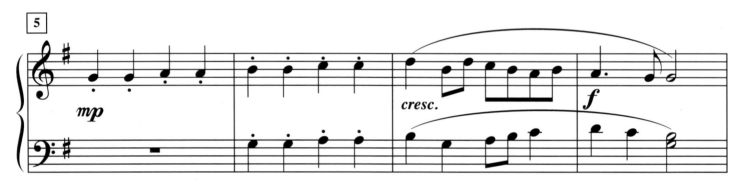

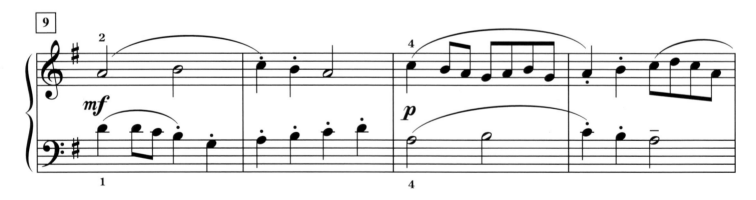

Menuet in D Minor

Jean-Baptiste Lully (1632–1687)

Keys to this piece:

- Both hands are equally important. Bring out the LH answering *motive*.
- Sometimes the hands play contrasting touches at the same time.
- Add *mordent* (✹) and *trills* (⤳) second time only.

7

Menuett in A Minor

Johann Krieger (1652–1735)

Keys to this piece:

Both hands are equally important.

Dynamics are varied when the *motive* repeats.

Add *trills* (𝄐) second time only.

Moderato (♩ = 108–120)

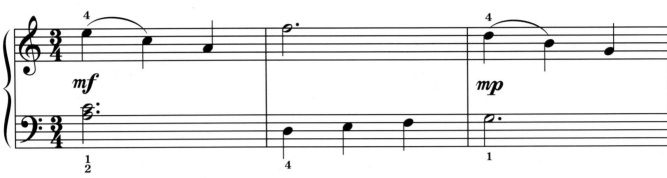

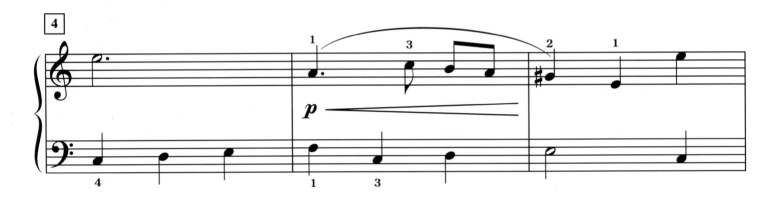

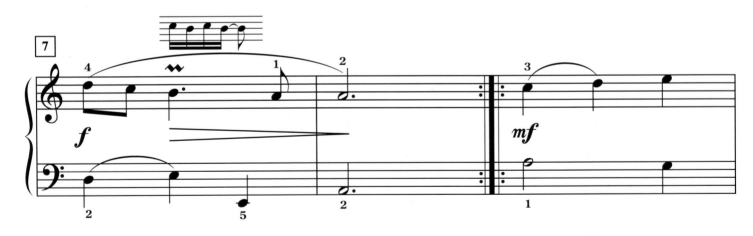

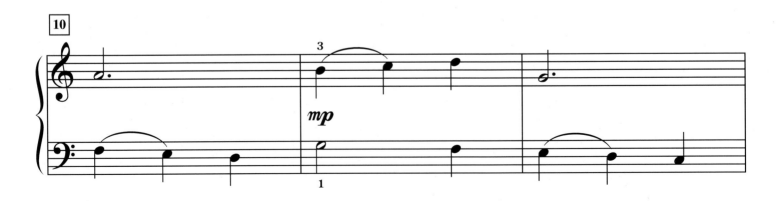

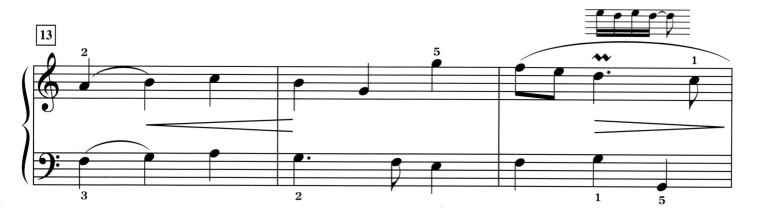

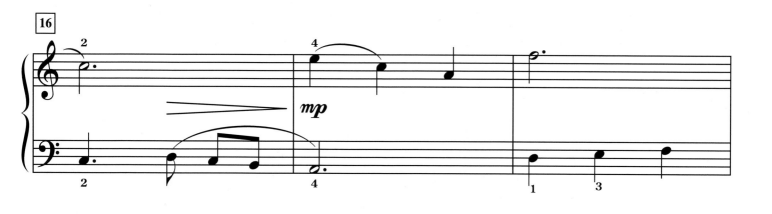

Gigue

Georg Philipp Telemann (1681–1767)

Keys to this piece:

Crisply detach the eighth notes in both hands, except where slurs are indicated.

Add *trills* (ꞷ) second time only.

The tempo must be steady with a slight *ritardando* at the final cadence the second time.

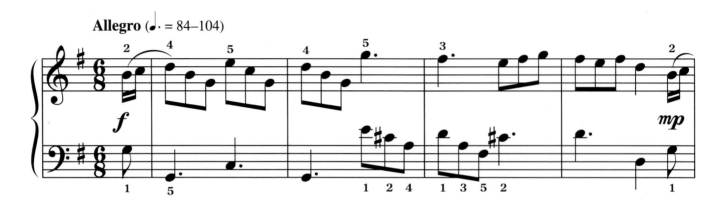

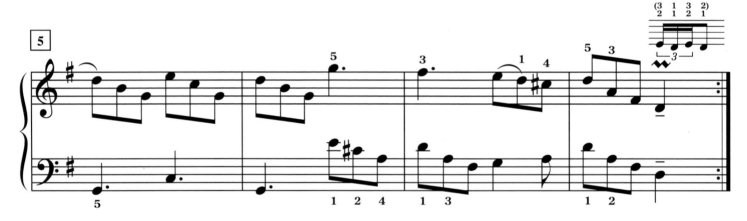

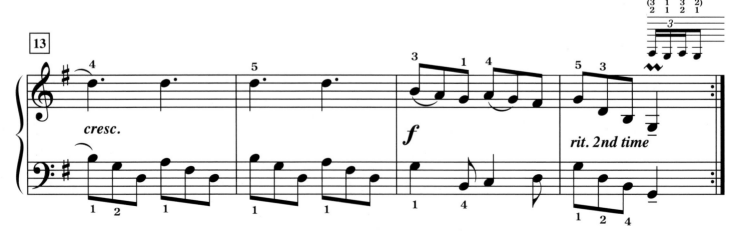

Chorale from *Notebook for Anna Magdalena*

Johann Sebastian Bach (1685–1750)

Keys to this piece:

- The melody is in the RH, but both hands are important.

- Stepwise motion is usually *legato;* leaps are usually detached.

- Vary dynamics and add *trill* (✹) in m. 7 second time only.

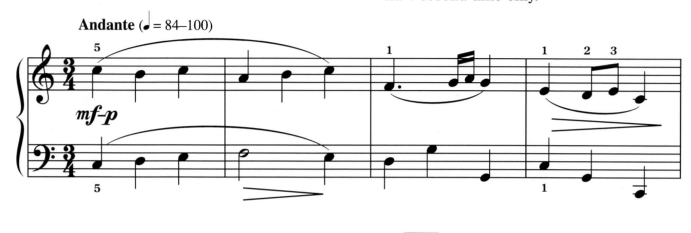

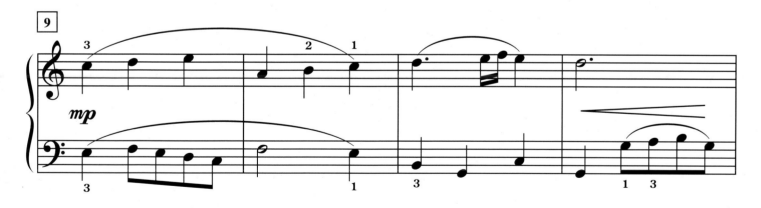

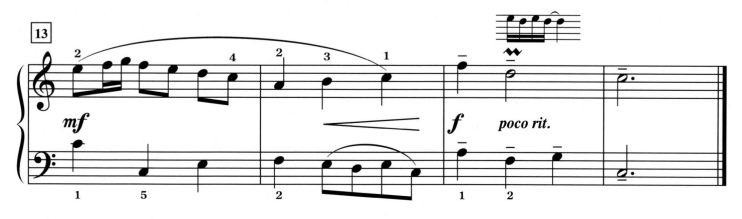

11

Aylesford* Piece

George Frideric Handel (1685–1759)

Keys to this piece:

🔑 Both hands are equally important. Bring out the LH answering *motive*.

🔑 Observe the *articulation* and place a slight emphasis on the downbeat to highlight the strong rhythmic character.

🔑 Dynamics often change when *motives* repeat.

Animato (♩= 84–100)

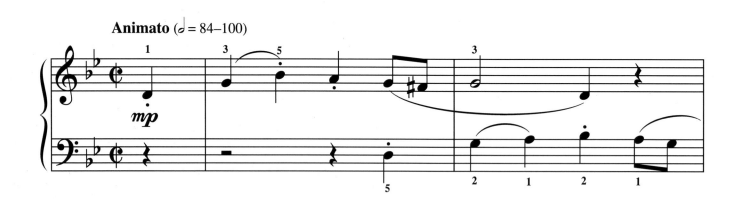

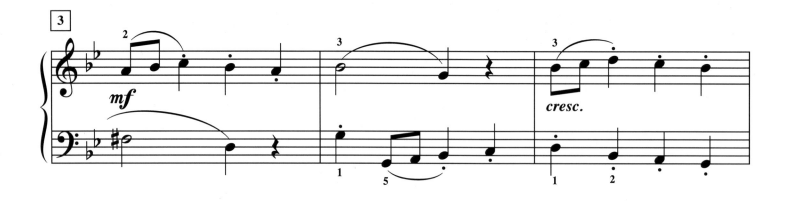

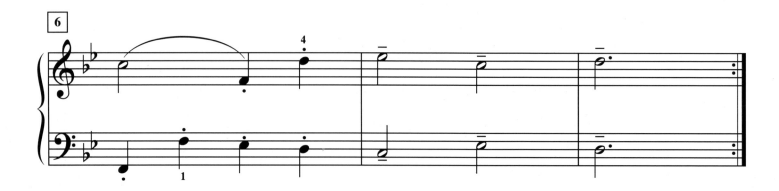

*Aylesford is said to be the oldest town in England.

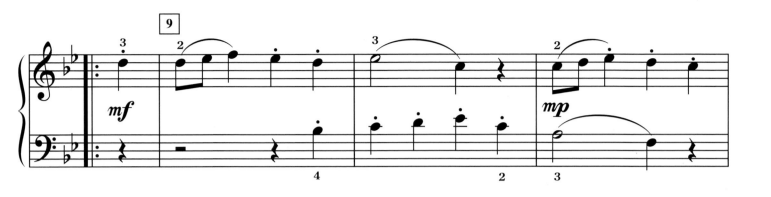

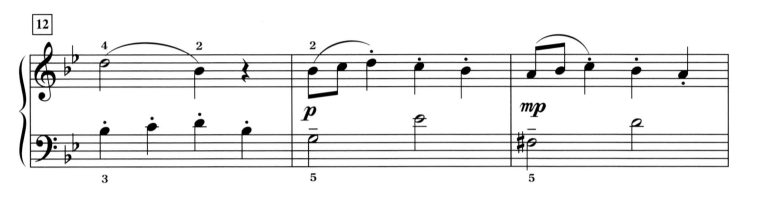

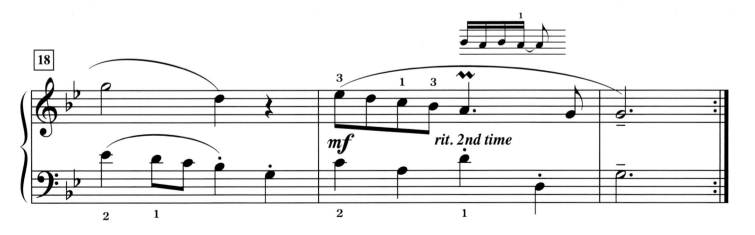

THE CLASSICAL PERIOD
(1750–1820)

Composers
Ludwig van Beethoven (1770–1827)

Muzio Clementi (1752–1832)

Carl Czerny (1791–1857)

Anton Diabelli (1781–1858)

Franz Joseph Haydn (1732–1809)

Friedrich Kuhlau (1786–1832)

Wolfgang Amadeus Mozart (1756–1791)

Keyboard Instruments
Harpsichord

Pianoforte

The pianoforte was invented by Bartolommeo Cristofori in 1700. It was originally called "gravicembalo col piano e forte," which means "harpsichord with soft and loud."

Typical Forms
Sonatina

Sonata

Concerto

Minuet & Trio

Rondo

Theme & Variations

KEYS TO STYLISTIC MASTERY

Melody

Influenced by vocal music.

⚷ Sing the melody as you play; follow the rise and fall of the line to shape it.

Grouped into two- and four-measure phrases.

⚷ Lift your wrists at phrase endings and breathe.

Often based on short *motives* with two- or three-note slurs.

⚷ As you *articulate* short *motives,* create a long line.

Rhythm

Frequent changes in the subdivisions of the beat from ♩ to   and

⚷ Write the counting in the music and count aloud (1+2+, etc.).

Rests and fermatas often add humor and drama.

⚷ Observe, count and feel the rests and fermatas.

Harmony

Chord patterns in *closely related keys;* themes often repeated in different keys.

⚷ Determine the key at the beginning and end of each section and when themes repeat.

Surprise harmonies and *non-chord tones* used to enhance musical expression.

⚷ Listen for the notes or harmonies that add color to the music. Highlight these notes by taking a little time on them.

✤ Tempo

Must be steady.

🔑 Learn the music using the metronome.

✤ Texture

Single melody line against a solid or broken chord accompaniment.

🔑 First **block** any broken chords.

🔑 Generally, keep the accompaniment two dynamic levels softer than the melody.

✤ Technique

Many scale patterns and solid and broken chords.

🔑 Practice the notes and fingerings of scales and chords using different dynamics and touches.

Singing melody must project above a softer accompaniment.

🔑 Use arm weight to project the melody. Keep fingers close to the keys to play broken chords softly.

Sound should be clear with precise *articulation* and varied touches.

🔑 Keep fingertips firm for a clear sound.

🔑 Use a small down-up wrist motion on the slurs.

🔑 Observe when there are different touches in each hand.

✤ Dynamics

***Motives* often repeat, suggesting different dynamic levels.**

🔑 Vary the dynamics when the motive repeats.

Range should be between *pp* and *ff* with sharp dynamic contrast.

🔑 *Piano* must be clear and elegant; *forte* should be full and bright.

✤ Expression

Different themes reflect contrasting moods.

🔑 Determine the mood or **character** of each section. In the music, write a word or draw an image that describes the mood.

✤ Pedal

Light touches of *damper pedal* on long notes.

🔑 Listen for long notes that will sing out more with a light touch of pedal.

✤ Additional Considerations

Drama and contrast highlighted by thinking orchestrally.

🔑 In the score, write the instruments you can imagine playing the music.

Influence of Classical dance steps.

🔑 Look for two- and three-note slurs and imagine dancers bowing to each other.

Bagatelle

Anton Diabelli (1781–1858)

🔑 Keys to this piece:

🗝 Play the LH two dynamic levels softer than the RH throughout.

🗝 Shape the vocal melody to follow the rise and fall of the line; it must always project above the accompaniment.

🗝 First begin without pedal, then use light touches of pedal *(half pedal)* or *finger pedal* to blend the melody with the broken chord accompaniment.

Allegretto (♩. = 69–80)

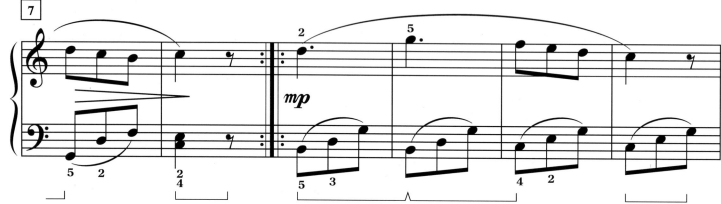

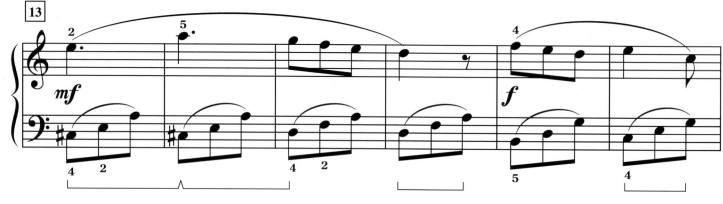

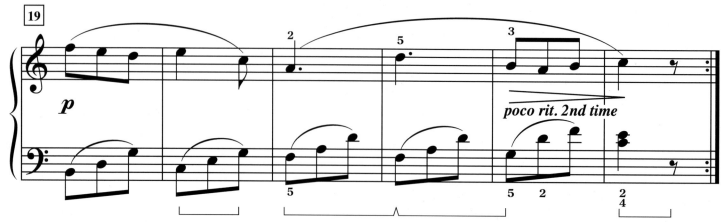

16

Kanzonette in C Major

Christian Gottlob Neefe (1748–1798)

Keys to this piece:

- The melody shows the influence of vocal music.

- The phrase lengths follow a typical classical structure: two measures, two measures, four measures.

- Vary dynamics for repeating *motives* and play *ornaments* both times.

17

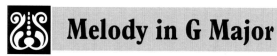

Melody in G Major

Carl Czerny (1791–1857)

Allegretto (♩. = 80–88)

Op. 777, No. 8

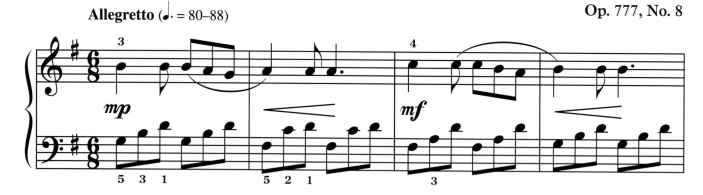

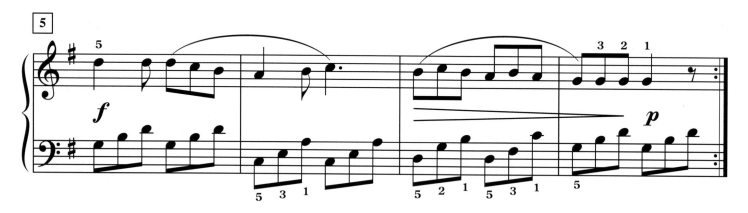

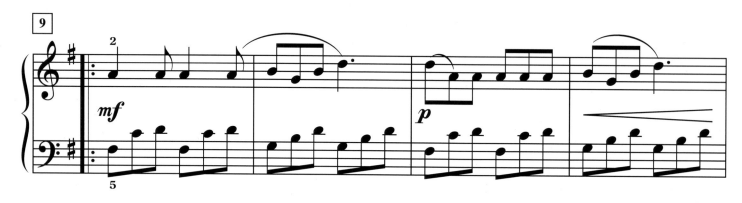

The first movements of sonatinas or sonatas are most typically in sonata-allegro form. In *Miniature Sonatina* (page 20), you can see the basic three sections of sonata-allegro form: exposition, development and recapitulation.

Exposition

Two or more themes are presented. The first theme is in the *tonic* key center and the second theme is in a different key.

Development

Themes are developed, combined or shortened; they appear in different keys.

Recapitulation

Themes are presented again. This time, both themes are in the *tonic* key.

Practice Tip

When learning sonatinas, practice similar themes (from the exposition, development and recapitulation) *one after another*. This will help facilitate memory.

Teachers may wish to have students imagine an interesting story line with characters to illustrate each section of a sonatina or sonata movement. This type of activity will help a student understand this style and perform it with more musical conviction.

Miniature Sonatina

Dennis Alexander (b. 1947)

🎼 Keys to this piece:

🗝 This sonatina is in sonata-allegro form.

🗝 The music contains contrasting dynamics and moods.

🗝 Precise *articulation* and varied touches are essential for an artistic performance.

Allegro (♩ = 92–108)
Exposition

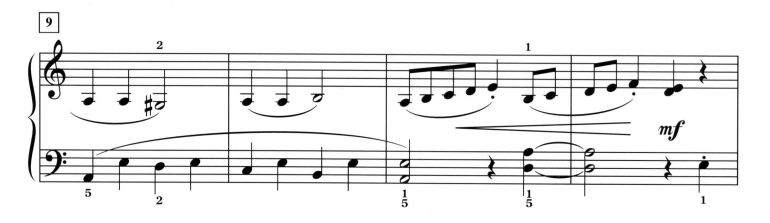

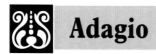

Adagio

Daniel Steibelt (1765–1823)

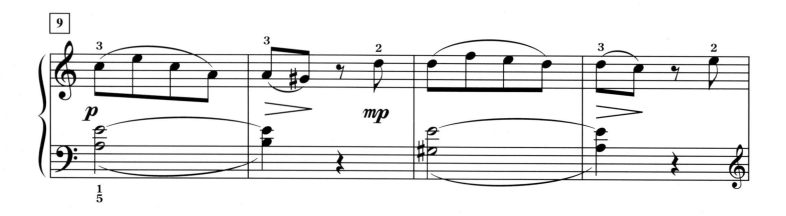

Keys to this piece:

- The melody is based on short slurs that must be linked to create a long line. The accompaniment must always be much softer.

- Repeating *motives* suggest different dynamic levels.

- Notice how the rhythms and harmonies in the accompaniment affect the melodic shaping and *character*.

Adagio (♩ = 72–80)

German Dance in G Major

Franz Joseph Haydn (1732–1809)

Keys to this piece:

- The music is written in balanced four-measure phrases.

- The melody is based on melodic turns, scale patterns and a broken chord; it must project above the LH accompaniment.

- The dance rhythm must be steady with a lively, robust feeling.

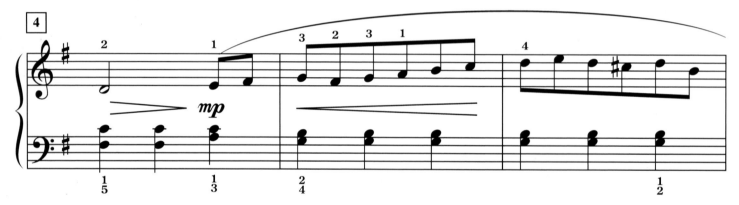

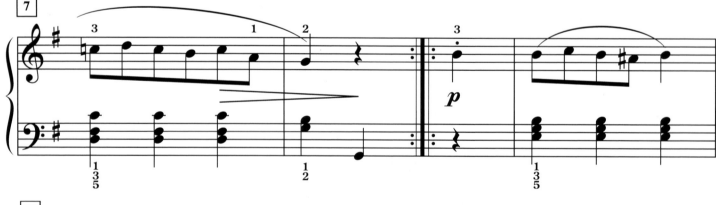

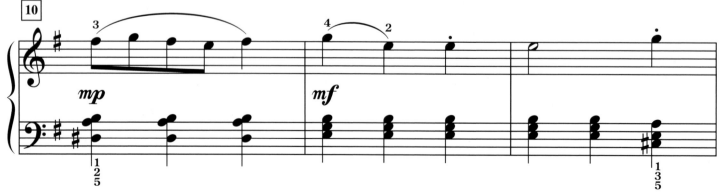

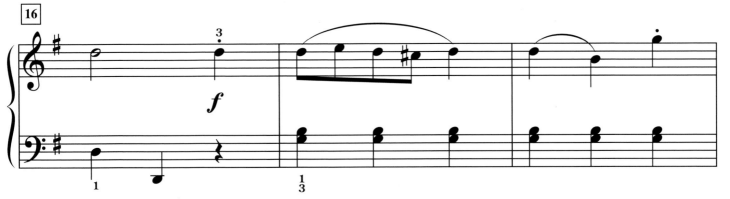

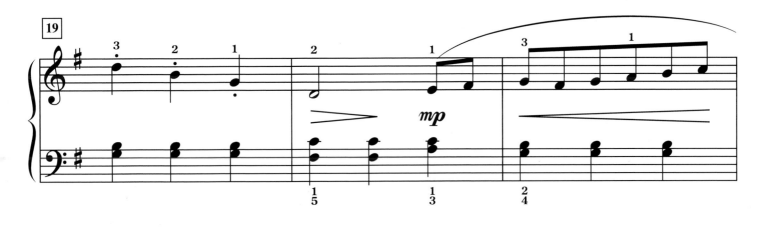

THE ROMANTIC PERIOD

(1820–1880)

Composers

Johannes Brahms (1833–1897)

Frédéric Chopin (1810–1849)

Edvard Grieg (1843–1907)

Cornelius Gurlitt (1820–1901)

Franz Liszt (1811–1886)

Felix Mendelssohn (1809–1847)

Franz Schubert (1797–1828)

Robert Schumann (1810–1856)

Peter Ilyich Tchaikovsky (1840–1893)

Keyboard Instruments

Piano

Organ

Typical Forms

Character piece

Etude

Concerto

Dance

Theme & Variations

KEYS TO STYLISTIC MASTERY

Melody

The prominent feature; may be a single note, two notes, or part of a chord.

⚷ The melody must project over the accompaniment. Bring out the top note of double notes and chords.

Often expressive and emotional.

⚷ Sing as you play, exaggerating the melodic shaping, and breathing like a singer.

Rhythm

Often more complex patterns than in Baroque and Classical periods.

⚷ Write the counting in the music where needed.

Harmony

Thicker harmonies and *sonorities* support the melody to create richer colors.

⚷ Listen for good balance between the hands especially when the texture is complex.

Tempo

Greater flexibility than in Baroque and Classical periods; *tempo rubato* (robbed time)—the melody "bends" the tempo over a steady accompaniment.

⚷ First learn with a steady tempo. Listen for places where slightly "bending" the tempo might be effective.

 Texture

Varied accompaniments create different textures and moods.

 Practice the accompaniment alone. Decide how it affects the *character* of the music.

Technique

Free upper arm motion needed to cover the full range of the piano.

 Practice leaps and changes of registers to feel the full range of motion.

LH accompaniment often has a two-voice texture with the lower note emphasized.

 First learn the LH accompaniment using two hands. Slightly bring out the LH bass note. Then practice the LH alone, imitating the balance you achieved with two hands.

Dynamics

Expanded dynamic range to match the increased capabilities of the piano. The piano is larger than it was in the Classical period.

 Pace the long *crescendos* and *diminuendos* so that you gradually get louder or softer.

Expression

Great intensity of expression represents a wide range of emotions.

 Determine the moods of the piece and write descriptive words in the score. Show these moods in your playing.

Descriptive titles often indicate a story inspired by literature, folklore, the supernatural or a strong sense of *nationalism.*

 Learn about the title of each piece and why it was composed to help you tell the music's story.

Pedal

Use of the *damper pedal* to create colors and blend the melody and harmony.

 When adding pedal, listen for smooth pedal changes immediately *after* the note where pedal is indicated. This is called *syncopated* or *legato pedal.*

Additional Considerations

Variety of new forms and genres of composition.

 Learn about the type of piece, and discover its character. Analyze the form to help you understand and memorize it.

Waltz

Emil Breslaur (1836–1899)

Keys to this piece:

- The graceful, dance-like melody is the prominent feature.

- The LH accompaniment is in two voices, with emphasis on the lowest note.

- The music reflects the elegant dance steps of the waltz: three steps of equal length, with the first one being slightly heavier.

28

Tender Thoughts

Dennis Alexander (b. 1947)

Keys to this piece:

🔑 The expressive melody is in a vocal style.

🔑 The melody and harmony blend together to create rich colors when using the *damper pedal*.

🔑 Take a little extra time on the highpoints in the melody and at the ends of phrases.

Moderato e molto espressivo (♩ = 92–100)
(Moderately, and with much expression)

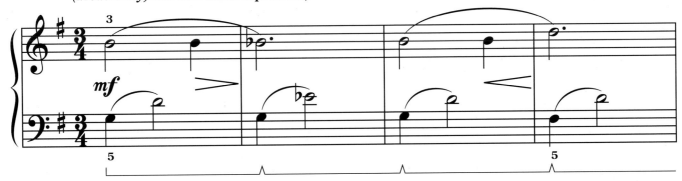

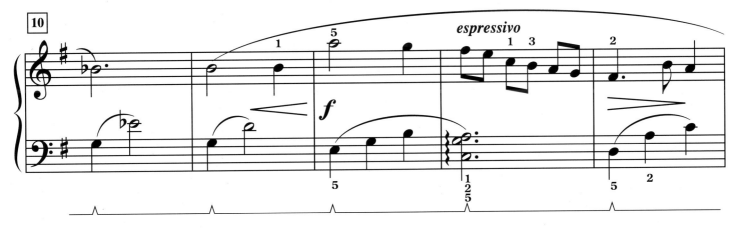

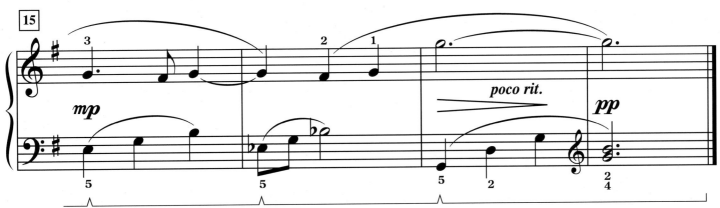

29

Little Piece

Robert Schumann (1810–1856)

Keys to this piece:

- The expressive melody shows a strong vocal influence.

- The LH accompaniment contains a *countermelody* that should be connected and shaped, but played softer than the RH.

- Use light touches of *damper pedal* to blend the sound at the ends of the phrases.

Op. 68, No. 5

Elegy

Carl Reinecke (1824–1910)

Andante con moto ($\bullet$ = 104–116)
(Walking tempo, with motion)

March

Cornelius Gurlitt (1820–1901)

Op. 140, No. 1

Vivace, ma non troppo (♩ = 100–112)
(Quickly, but not too fast)

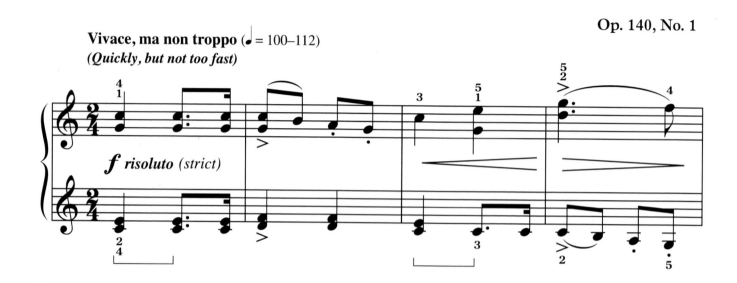

Melody

François Thomé (1850–1909)

Keys to this piece:

- The expressive melody must project above the LH accompaniment.
- The changing LH harmonies help support the expressive RH melodic shaping.
- Use the *damper pedal* to blend the melody and harmony to create a dreamy mood.

Andantino espressivo (♩ = 116–132)
(Moving quickly along, expressively)

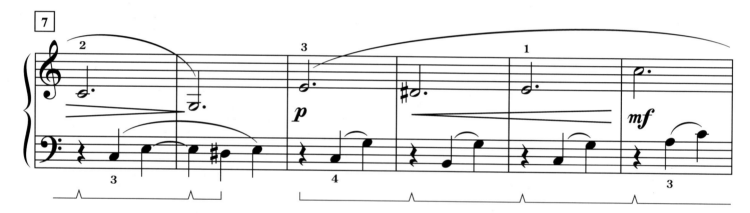

34

THE IMPRESSIONIST PERIOD

(1890–1930)

Composers
Claude Debussy (1862–1918)

Maurice Ravel (1875–1937)

Keyboard Instruments
Piano

Typical Forms
Character Piece

Prelude

Dance

Suite

KEYS TO STYLISTIC MASTERY

Melody

Often based on *pentatonic* or *whole tone* scales.

○—ᴛ Play the melody to determine if it is based on one of these scales.

Often found in the top note of a 4th or 5th; in the middle register, surrounded by two outer layers of sound; passes from one hand to the other.

○—ᴛ Find the melody and highlight it with a pencil or marker. Practice the melody alone.

Rhythm

Changes from duple to triple ♪♪♪ subdivisions of the beat within the measure.

○—ᴛ Tap the rhythm to feel the contrasting subdivisions. Learn the music with the metronome set to the quarter note.

Harmony

Chords with no 3rd or an added 2nd; also augmented chords and 7th and 9th chords.

○—ᴛ Write in the names of the chords to simplify memorization.

Tempo

Changes and *ritardandos* specifically indicated by the composer.

○—ᴛ First learn the piece keeping a steady tempo. Then carefully pace the *ritardandos* and tempo changes.

⌇ Texture

Open 4ths and 5ths or chords that shift in parallel blocks to different pitches.

🗝 Practice these blocked intervals or chords alone. As the hand shape stays fixed, keep the arm loose.

⌇ Technique

Different arm gestures on chords to help achieve muted colors.

🗝 Play chords by depressing the keys from the arm; stroke keys with the pads of your fingers. Gently pull the forearm towards your body.

Smooth weight transfer for broken chords and melodies divided between the hands.

🗝 Practice these chords and melodies, making them sound like one hand is playing.

Top notes of blocked 4th and 5ths must be emphasized.

🗝 Bring out the top note of blocked intervals by *voicing* them.

⌇ Dynamics

The full range of the instrument is utilized, from *ppp* to *ff*; many levels of soft dynamics.

🗝 Be sure to play using the very specific dynamic markings. Carefully differentiate *mp*, *p*, *pp* and *ppp*.

⌇ Expression

Very specific marks of *articulation,* particularly *tenutos, portatos, staccatos,* slurs and different kinds of accents.

🗝 Exaggerate the suggested articulations to help project the character of the music.

⌇ Pedal

Variety of pedal: *legato pedal,* changing with the bass note, and/or blending harmonies over several measures.

🗝 Use the pedaling suggested. If none is given, experiment with full and *half pedal.* Keep the pedal down on long bass notes.

Una corda (u.c.) pedal is often indicated.

🗝 First learn without the *u.c.* to get as soft a tone as possible. Then add *u.c.* where indicated and experiment with other places it might be effective.

⌇ Additional Considerations

Inspiration from impressionistic paintings, nature, the world of fantasy, and Eastern sounds and colors.

🗝 Look at the titles and listen to how the composer creates the colors of a painting, the sounds of nature, or tells a story. Listen for the Eastern scales and the sounds imitating bells and gongs.

Glistening Willows

Dennis Alexander (b. 1947)

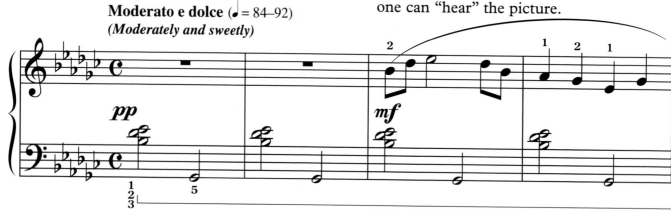

Keys to this piece:

- The melody is based on a *pentatonic scale* and parallel 4ths, giving it an Eastern sound.

- LH harmonies comprise open 5ths or triads with added 6ths.

- The inspiration of nature is evident as one can "hear" the picture.

Moderato e dolce ($\bullet$ = 84–92)
(*Moderately and sweetly*)

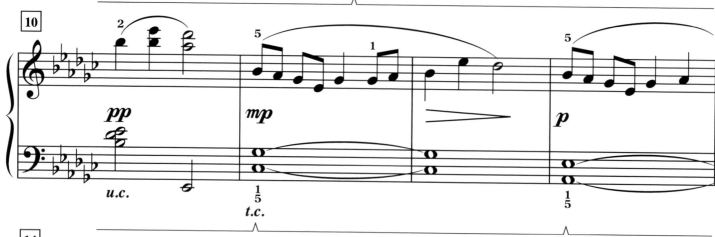

38

Osaka Castle Gardens

Dennis Alexander (b. 1947)

Keys to this piece:

This piece contains open 4ths that move in parallel motion. The **pentatonic** melody passes from one hand to the other.

Blend the sounds by keeping the **damper pedal** down.

Andantino (♩ = 104–112)

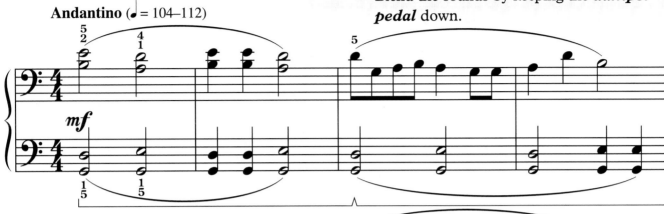

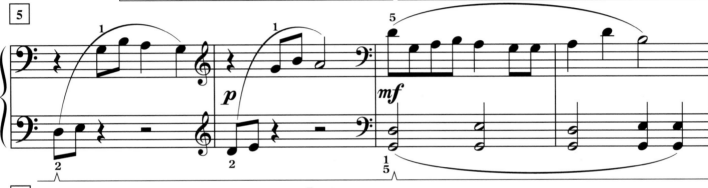

39

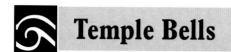

Temple Bells

Dennis Alexander (b. 1947)

Keys to this piece:

🔑 The melody uses two *pentatonic scales:* one on white keys and one on black keys.

🔑 The harmony is based on shifting open 5ths, imitating the sounds of bells and gongs.

40

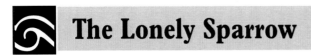

The Lonely Sparrow

Dennis Alexander (b. 1947)

Keys to this piece:

- The *whole-tone* melody passes between the hands.
- Hold the *damper pedal* down to create a blending of colors.
- Inspiration of nature is suggested by the title.

Andante con espressione (♩ = 80–92)
(Walking tempo, with expression)

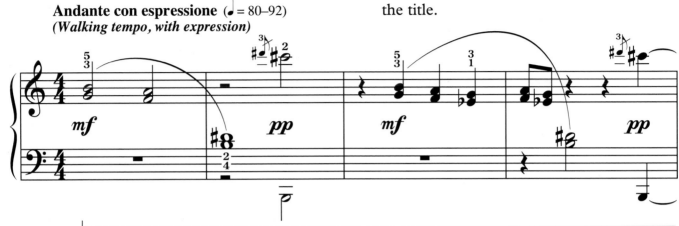

lowest F on piano

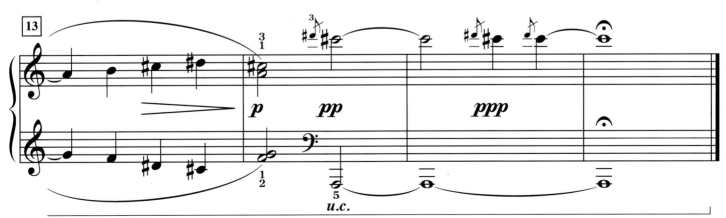

u.c.

41

THE CONTEMPORARY PERIOD

(1900–present)

Composers

Béla Bartók (1881–1945)

Aaron Copland (1900–1991)

Alberto Ginastera (1915–1983)

Alexander Gretchaninoff (1864–1956)

Dmitri Kabalevsky (1904–1987)

Aram Khachaturian (1903–1978)

Sergei Prokofiev (1891–1953)

Dmitri Shostakovich (1906–1975)

Igor Stravinsky (1882–1971)

Heitor Villa-Lobos (1887–1959)

Keyboard Instruments

Piano

Organ

Electronic Keyboard

Synthesizer

Digital Piano

Typical Forms and Compositional Techniques

12-Tone

Aleatoric

Free Form

Fantasy

Dance

Sonata

Character Piece

KEYS TO STYLISTIC MASTERY

Melody

Unpredictable or irregular phrase lengths.

⚷ Make note of the lengths of phrases to assist you in interpretation and memorization.

Shape is often jagged using very narrow or very wide intervals; often based on non-traditional scales.

⚷ Plan fingering carefully to play these less familiar patterns.

Rhythm

Greater use of irregular meters like $\frac{5}{4}$ or $\frac{7}{8}$.

⚷ Circle all meter changes. Look for the rhythmic groupings that will assist you in hearing the rhythm easily. Count aloud as you play.

Jazz rhythms with characteristic accents and *syncopation.*

⚷ Write in the counting. Bring out weak beats that are emphasized.

Harmony

Lack of a strong feeling of key center or tonality. Use of *bitonality* or *atonality*.

⚷ Look for any *tonal center* and write in the key names.

Chords made up of 4ths, 5ths or clusters of three or more adjacent notes to create a *dissonant* sound.

⚷ Identify intervals used in the chords.

Tempo

Changes indicated by the composer.

 Circle all tempo changes.

Texture

Very specific *articulation* and varied touches; sound may range from muted to very percussive.

 Listen for the desired quality of sound needed for the piece.

Technique

Hand shape must adjust to narrow or wide intervals and unusual chord shapes.

 Notice the intervals used and expand or contract your hand to adjust.

Dynamics

The full range of the instrument is utilized, from *ppp* to *fff*—a wide dynamic spectrum.

 Observe the composer's specific dynamics.

Expression

Titles tell a story; pieces express a wide range of emotions; sounds reflect the *character*.

 Look at the title and determine the mood or moods in the score. If there is no descriptive title, listen to the sounds you are creating and decide what mood is conveyed.

Additional Considerations

Use of unconventional pianistic movements such as playing with the palm or forearm, or tapping the wood of the piano.

 Listen to the interesting sounds created by these unusual ways of playing the piano.

Big physical gestures and motions needed to accommodate extreme registers of the piano.

 Time your motions according to the tempo; sharp gestures for faster tempos, and graceful gestures for slower tempos.

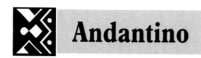

Andantino

Igor Stravinsky (1882–1971)

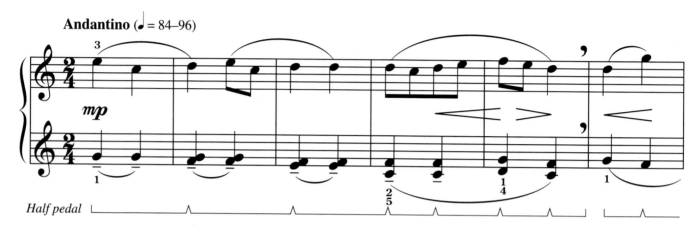

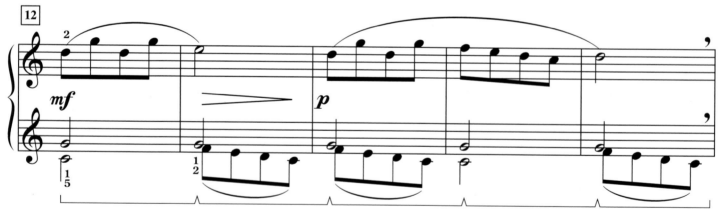

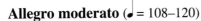

Hungarian Folk Dance

Béla Bartók (1881–1945)

Keys to this piece:

- There are frequent changes of tempo indicated by the composer.

- The composer has provided very specific and contrasting **articulations.**

- The rhythm and harmonies are based on Hungarian folk songs.

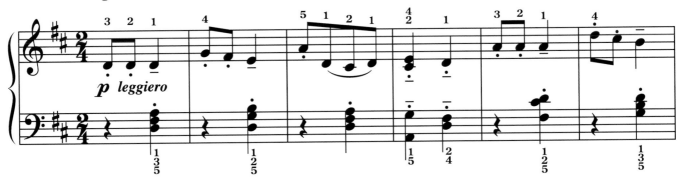

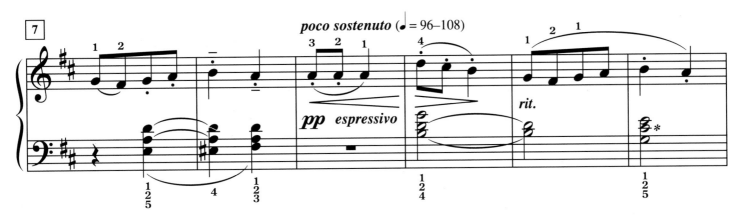

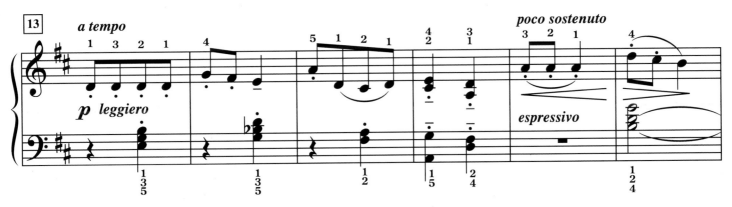

* *C-natural in some editions.*

45

The Shepherd's Flute

Samuel Maykapar (1867–1938)

46

The Chinese Doll

Vladimir Rebikov (1866–1920)

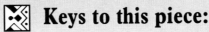

Keys to this piece:

- The *pentatonic scale* is used in mm. 1–8 and 17–24.

- *Dissonance* is created by *bitonality* in mm. 9–16 (LH = C major, RH = D-flat major).

- The composer has provided very specific and varied articulations.

Allegretto (♩ = 84–96)

47

Slovak Peasant's Dance

Béla Bartók (1881–1945)

Keys to this piece:

- The melody is based on the Aeolian mode, typical in Hungarian folk songs.
- LH intervals in the accompaniment create *dissonance*.
- Very specific *articulation* is used to highlight the strong rhythmic character.

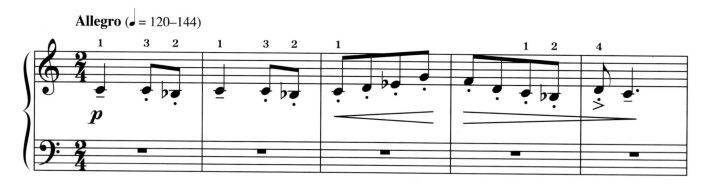

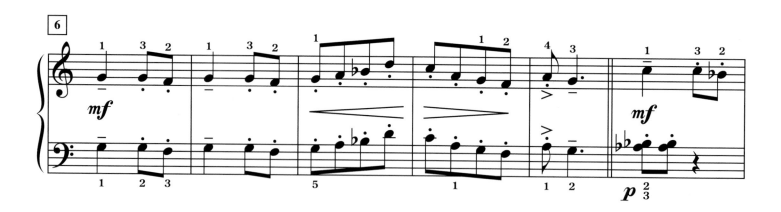

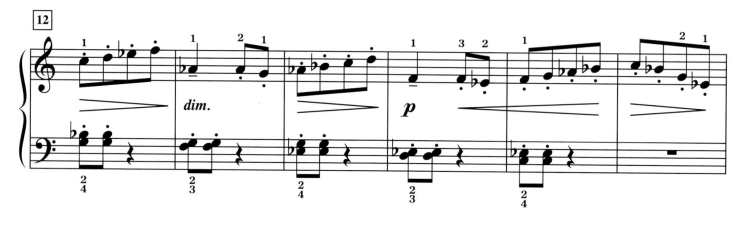

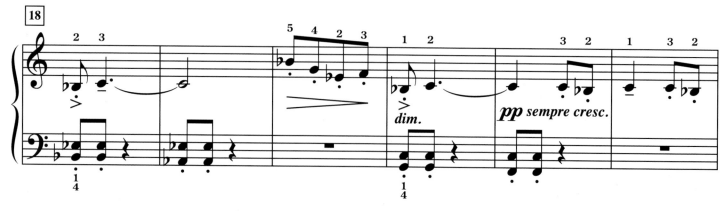

Zany Zebras

Dennis Alexander (b. 1947)

Keys to this piece:

- This piece is **bitonal:** the RH is in A minor; the LH is in D-flat major.

- Unusual **sonorities** are achieved by using the side of the hand to play clusters of notes.

- Dynamics and **articulation** markings are very precisely indicated by the composer.

ABOUT THE COMPOSERS

Dennis Alexander (b. 1947) is one of North America's most prolific and popular composers of educational piano music. He taught piano and piano pedagogy at the university level for over 24 years and currently resides in southern California where he teaches and composes music for students.

Johann Sebastian Bach (1685–1750) is considered to be the Baroque period's most supreme composer. Bach was a master of compositional forms including dances, inventions, fugues and variations. The German composer was an expert organist and improviser, who wrote new music each week for the church service.

Béla Bartók (1881–1945) was one of the most influential composers of the 20th century. His piano music, most particularly *Mikrokosmos*, provides a textbook of 20th-century compositional techniques. Bartók, a professor at the Budapest Academy in Hungary, married one of his students with whom he performed two-piano recitals in the United States and Russia.

Emil Breslaur (1836–1899) was a German piano teacher, a religious instructor and rabbi for the Jewish community in Cottbus, Germany. He founded and directed a German conservatory that trained piano teachers. Breslaur, dedicated to the art of teaching, founded the German Music Teacher Association in Berlin in 1879.

Carl Czerny (1791–1857) studied with Ludwig van Beethoven and was the teacher of Franz Liszt. In addition to composing, he read books about science and classical antiquity, wrote essays and plays, and spoke Czech, Italian, French and German. Czerny composed over 1000 works— mostly exercises—but also sonatinas, sonatas, dances, chamber music and sacred choral works.

Anton Diabelli (1781–1858) was an Austrian composer and music publisher. His keyboard sonatinas and the collections *Pleasures of Youth*, Op.163, and *Melodious Pieces*, Op.149, are favorites among young pianists for technical development.

Cornelius Gurlitt (1820–1901) was a German composer and conductor. He is acclaimed for his charming and spirited piano duets. His smaller piano works are an important and beloved part of the teaching literature for the developing young pianist.

George Frideric Handel (1685–1759) was a naturalized English composer who was born in Germany. He is considered to be one of the greatest vocal and instrumental composers of the Baroque period. Handel's fame rests primarily on his operas, cantatas, and oratorios (most notably, *Messiah*). He also composed many works for keyboard. Like Bach, he was an excellent keyboard performer and a master at improvisation.

Franz Joseph Haydn (1732–1809) was an Austrian composer whose long musical career spanned the Classical period. Haydn was a popular conductor and composer among the music-loving aristocracy of Europe, especially the Esterházy family—a wealthy Hungarian family famous for their patronage of the arts—with whom Haydn remained in musical service for over 30 years. Haydn was a prolific composer of church music, string quartets, and is renowned as the "Father of the Symphony."

Johann Krieger (1652–1735) was a German composer and organist. Handel considered him to be one of the best composers of organ music. In addition to his keyboard works, he wrote many secular and sacred songs and cantatas.

Jean-Baptiste Lully (1632–1687) was Italian by birth but lived in France where he became friends with Louis XIV. He received the title of "Master of Music for the Royal Family." Lully was a teacher, violinist, dancer, comedian and composer of opera, ballets and church music.

Samuel Maykapar (1867–1938) was a Russian composer and concert pianist. He studied at the St. Petersburg Conservatory and also in Vienna. In addition to a concert career, he was a professor at the St. Petersburg Conservatory. Maykapar is best known for his piano pieces, especially his works for students.

Christian Gottlob Neefe (1748–1798) was a German composer, teacher and organist who also studied law. He taught piano, organ and composition to Beethoven. Neefe composed operas, operettas and works for solo piano.

Vladimir Rebikov (1866–1920) is known as the "Father of Russian Modernism." He was fascinated by the 20th-century style of expressionism, which explores how music can reflect the psychology and extreme emotions of people.

Carl Reinecke (1824–1910) was a German music educator, performer, and conductor. He was a brilliant teacher who was highly respected for inspiring high standards of performance from his students. In addition to writing compositions for piano, Reinecke was also a gifted poet and painter.

Robert Schumann (1810–1856) was a German composer who is considered one of the most original in the Romantic era. Many of his pieces are musical stories or portraits revealing the strong influence literature had on his life. He went to the university to study law, but he left to pursue his true passion—music. He married his piano teacher's daughter, Clara Wieck, who also was a great pianist and composer.

Daniel Steibelt (1765–1823) was a German composer and pianist. While in Vienna, he competed in a piano contest with Beethoven, and lost. His works include many compositions for piano, several operas and ballets, and songs.

Igor Stravinsky (1882–1971) was born in Russia, lived in Paris for many years and became a United States citizen in 1945. Stravinsky, at his parents' insistence, went to university to study law. He eventually, however, chose to follow his dream of becoming a composer. Stravinsky is best known for his ballet music, but he also wrote orchestral and chamber music as well as opera and piano music.

Georg Philipp Telemann (1681–1767) was a German composer, whose works include opera, church music, songs, keyboard compositions and instrumental music. By age 10, he taught himself to play many instruments. At age 20, Telemann went to university to study law. He organized concerts and wrote books to make performance and composition more understandable to the general public.

Francois Thomé (1850–1909), a French teacher and composer, studied at the Paris Conservatory. He is best known for his piano pieces. He also composed two operas, several ballets, choral works and many songs.

GLOSSARY

accent (♩ ♩)

Emphasis on a note or chord.

articulation

The manner in which notes are attacked or released. Articulation signs show length of notes and groupings of notes, e.g., staccato, legato, portato, accent.

atonality

Music that does not have a tonal center.

bagatelle

A short piece, usually for piano.

bitonality

Two or more tonal centers occurring at the same time.

block

To play as a chord or cluster rather than as a broken chord.

cadence

The melodic or harmonic ending of a phrase, section or movement.

character

The "personality" of a piece of music.

chorale

A hymn tune or sacred melody.

closely related keys

Chords and harmonies that share common tones with a tonal center. The most closely related keys are either a fourth or a fifth up from the tonal center or a minor third down. For example, the closely related keys of C major are F major, G major and A minor.

countermelody

A melody in another voice that is different from the main melody. This often creates a duet.

counterpoint

Music that combines two or more melody lines. Literally, it means "note against note."

damper pedal

The pedal on the right. When depressed, it lifts the dampers allowing the strings to vibrate freely. This sustains the sound until the pedal is lifted.

dissonance

Two or more notes that, when played together, sound like they disagree or clash.

etude

A piece that focuses on a specific technical problem such as scales, arpeggios, or octaves.

finger pedal

To hold down one or more notes with the fingers rather than with pedal.

half pedal

Depressing the damper pedal only half way to avoid an accumulation of too much sound or an unclear sound.

legato

Smooth and connected. Generally indicated by a slur (⌒).

legato pedal

Using the damper pedal to give the illusion of playing legato. In this book, it is indicated with a wedge that shows the pedal coming up, and immediately back down after the note is struck. Also called "syncopated pedaling" (└──∧──┘).

linear

Music that is horizontal (one note at a time), as opposed to vertical (chords).

menuet

A French country dance in moderate triple meter. It is also spelled *minuet* (English), *menuett* (German) or *minuetto* (Italian).

mordent (𝄽)

An ornament consisting of an alternation of the written note with the note immediately below it.

motive — A melodic or rhythmic musical figure that recurs throughout a composition. Sometimes spelled "motif."

nationalism — Loyalty and devotion to a country and the promotion of its culture. This is usually reflected in music through the use of folk tunes and dance.

non-chord tones — Tones that are foreign to the harmony and occur as melodic ornamentation. They create interesting tonal color and intensity.

ornaments — Decorative embellishments. They can be written by the composer or improvised by the performer. See *trill* and *mordent*.

pentatonic scale — The major scale without the 4th and 7th degrees. On the piano, it can be produced by playing the black keys only.

portato (♩ ♩) — Articulation that is halfway between legato and staccato.

sonorities — Richness and variety of sound.

staccato (♩ ♩) — Articulation that is short and detached.

syncopation — Shifting the accents to the normally weak beats of the measure.

syncopated pedal — See *legato pedal.*

tenuto (♩ ♩) — Hold the note for its full value.

terraced dynamics — An abrupt change of dynamics, instead of crescendos and diminuendos. It is often used in sequential patterns, and is typical of the Baroque and early Classical style.

tonal center — The main key in which a piece or section of a piece is written.

tonality — See *tonal center.*

tonic — The first note of a scale or key (keynote).

tre corde (t.c.) — A direction to release the left pedal, which moves the action to the left (on a grand piano) and causes the hammer to strike three strings (tre corde).

trill (〰) — An ornament consisting of an alternation of the written note with the note immediately above it; it can begin on the written pitch, or on the note above the written pitch, depending on the period.

una corda (u.c.) — A direction to use the left pedal, which moves the action to the right (on a grand piano) and causes the hammer to strike only one string (una corda) or two strings. On an upright piano, the hammers move closer to the strings. This causes the sound to be softer and changes the tone quality.

voicing — Bringing out or highlighting important notes from a melody or motive, such as the top note of a chord, or the upper or lower voice in a broken interval passage.

whole tone scale — A scale in which the octave is divided equally into six whole steps. C, D, E, F♯, G♯, A♯ or D♭, E♭, F, G, A, B

ABOUT THE AUTHORS

Ingrid Jacobson Clarfield

Ingrid Jacobson Clarfield, Professor of Piano and Coordinator of the Piano Department at Westminster Choir College of Rider University in Princeton, New Jersey, is an active performer, clinician and author. She has presented pedagogy workshops, master classes, and lecture-recitals throughout the U.S. and Canada. Her students have won hundreds of awards at state, national and international competitions. Ms. Clarfield is co-author of *From Mystery to Mastery* and author of *Burgmüller, Czerny, Hanon: 32 Piano Studies Selected for Technique and Musicality.* Her editions of Debussy's *Golliwog's Cakewalk,* Beethoven's *Moonlight Sonata* and Chopin's *Nocturne in E-flat Major, Op. 9, No. 2,* are part of her *Artistic Preparation and Performance Series* (Alfred Music Publishing Co., Inc.). Her articles have been published in *The American Music Teacher, Keyboard Companion, Piano Life* and *Clavier.* Ms. Clarfield received her B.M. at Oberlin College where she studied with John Perry, and an M.M. from the Eastman School of Music.

Dennis Alexander

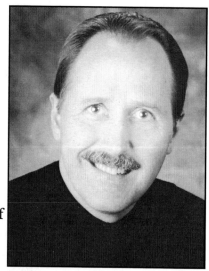

Since his affiliation with Alfred Music Publishing Company in 1986 as a composer and clinician, Dennis Alexander has earned an international reputation as one of North America's most prolific and popular composers of educational piano music for students at all levels. Professor Alexander retired from his position at the University of Montana in May 1996 where he taught piano and piano pedagogy for 24 years. He moved to Southern California in 1996 where he teaches privately while maintaining an active composing and touring schedule for Alfred Publishing Company.

Over the years, numerous organizations and state associations have commissioned him to write compositions. Many of his compositions are included in the national Federation of Music Study Clubs Festival required list, and his music is being performed by students throughout the United States, Canada, South Africa, Australia, Asia and Europe.